THE BASICS OF
WINNING
ROULETTE

J. Edward Allen

- Gambling Research Institute -
Cardoza Publishing

2015 New Edition

Copyright © 1985, 1993, 1998, 2002, 2015 by Cardoza Publishing
- All Rights Reserved -

Library of Congress Catalog Card No: 2015930689
ISBN 10: 1-58042-332-9   ISBN 13: 978-1-58042-332-8

Visit our website at www.cardozabooks.com or write
for a full list of books and advanced strategies.

CARDOZA PUBLISHING
PO Box 98115, Las Vegas, NV 89193
Toll-Free Phone (800)577-WINS
email: cardozabooks@aol.com
www.cardozabooks.com

Table of Contents

Illustrations & Charts

Illustrations

Charts

In the Chips!

I. Introduction

Roulette is a game that has fascinated and intrigued millions of players over the years. It's not only a leisurely game, but an exciting game as well.

You'll be playing the same game that has attracted kings and queens, prime ministers and statesmen, millionaires and captains of industry.

Roulette has a great variety of bets available, more than in any other casino table game. Betting choices may be paid off anywhere from even money to 35-1, and bets can overlap, with the same numbers covered in several ways.

Because of this factor, the game has attracted systems to beat it from the first time it was introduced. We'll show you the more popular ones and the pitfalls involved.

You'll find out details about both the American and European game, including the possible wagers and payoffs involved, so that you'll be able to play this most fascinating of games intelligently.

II. American Roulette

The Dealer

In American casinos, the game is run by one dealer. This is in contrast to the European version of roulette, in which several **croupiers** (the French term for dealer) are used, since the European game is played with a double layout, and more employees are needed to staff the table.

In American casinos, one dealer will suffice to run the game. Sometimes, if the game is particularly busy, the dealer may have an assistant, whose sole function will be to collect losing chips and stack them. This is the exception, not the rule.

The dealer has several duties. He or she will first change the player's cash into roulette chips. Each player will receive roulette chips of a different color from the other players' chips. These roulette chips are specially marked and have no intrinsic value away from the roulette table. The different colors make for a smoother game, since there will usually be a multitude of bets on the layout, and the only way the dealer will know how to make proper payoffs will be through the color of the chips.

In addition to changing cash for chips, the dealer runs the game. He keeps the wheel spinning, and he rolls a small white ball in the opposite direction, letting it spin until it falls into a slot on the wheel. This slot determines the winning number and other payoffs.

After a winning number is determined, the dealer collects all the losing chips first, then pays off the winning bets. The players then make new bets on the next spin of the ball, and the whole procedure is repeated.

There is usually a pitboss in the vicinity of the roulette wheel. He or she may supervise the play at the table and will be called upon if there is a dispute between the players and the dealer or between two or more players. Disputes rarely happen, though, since all players use different colored roulette chips.

Roulette Chips

As I mentioned, the chips are different colors than other casino chips and are marked differently. A player can't wager them at any other game in the casino. Players are also forbidden from taking these chips away from the roulette table. When they've finished playing, they must return all their chips to the dealer, who will pay off the player by exchanging these for casino chips, which can then be brought to the cashier's cage and exchanged for cash.

There is usually a standard value placed on the roulette chips. In the old days, before inflation, 10¢ or 25¢ chips were the standard. Today, it's hard to find a standard chip value less than $1. If a player gives the dealer a $20 bill, he or she will receive twenty chips, each with a value of $1.

The values of chips are not fixed, however. Suppose that a player came to the roulette table with a $100 bill and wanted each chip to be valued at $5. The player will request this valuation of the dealer, and the dealer, to be certain that no mistakes will be made later, will place a chip of the player's designated color on the outside rim of the wheel with a $5 marker on it, or a button to show that a stack of twenty chips is worth $100.

Where no chips are on the rim, everyone is playing with the standard value chips. These chips will come in enough colors, usually eight or ten different ones, to accommodate that many players. There will also be enough chairs at the roulette table for that number of players.

Players may change the valuation of their chips during the game. If a player won a lot of money, rather than continuing to bet with $1 chips and using handfuls of them, he could change the valuation of his chips to $5 each. He would simply have to turn them in to get them re-valued, or he might be given chips of a different color.

For bigger bets, such as $5, $25, or $100, the casino allows a player to use standard casino chips. Although players occasionally bet with standard casino chips or cash, this practice is not recommended since it can cause confusion about who owns those chips or that money. The vast majority of bets will be made with roulette chips.

When payoffs are made, the dealer *cuts* the chips, or breaks them into stacks. If the payoff is seventeen chips, for example, he'll cut a stack of twenty by taking three chips off the top. He'll then move the rest of the stack to the winner.

In contrast, in a European game, a **rake** is used to collect and pay out chips. In both games, after the number has come up, some kind of marker is placed on the layout to indicate the winning number before the losing chips are collected and the winning bets are paid off.

The American Wheel

The game of roulette depends on the spin of the wheel, an ornate device (see diagram below) that is approximately three feet in diameter and contains slots numbered from 1 to 36, plus a 0 and 00.

The bowl of the wheel, which takes up most of the wheel's space, contains numbered pockets. Above this bowl are eight metal buffers, some horizontal and some vertical, which are there to slow the ball as it spins counter to the wheel's motion, so that it will fall into a pocket in the most random manner possible.

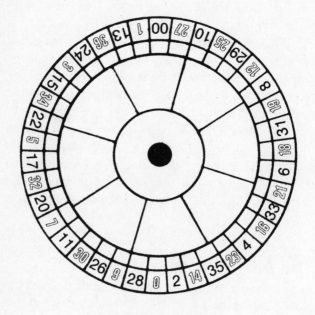

The American Wheel

When the ball falls into a pocket, that pocket corresponds to a particular number. The number determines which bets win and which lose for that spin of the wheel.

Each pocket is separated from its neighbors by metal dividers, known as **separators**. As the ball slows, it may fall into a pocket only to bounce up and into another pocket. Eventually inertia will cause it to remain in one pocket, and the number on that pocket wins for that spin.

There are thirty-six numbers in all, half in black and half in red, plus two extra numbers, the 0 and 00, which are in green. The numbers are not in consecutive order on the wheel. Rather, they are placed randomly, with red and black numbers alternating, except when interrupted by the 0 and 00.

With thirty-six numbers on the wheel, half are odd while half are even, half are black while half are red, and half are in the lower tier (1-18) while half are in the higher tier (19-36). All of these categories are possible bets: odd or even, red or black, high or low. As we shall later see, they are paid off at even money.

If there were only thirty-six numbers, the house would have no advantage over the player. Roulette would merely be a game of chance, without either side, the bettor or the casino, having an edge. The addition of the 0 and 00, however, gives the house a definite advantage of 5.26%. These could be called **house numbers**, because they are winning numbers for the house when the player bets on any of the even money propositions just mentioned, as well as when the player bets on other numbers and possibilities.

A gambler can bet on the 0 or 00 as numbers, just as he bets on any other numbers. In that case, though, there are thirty-eight possible numbers to bet on, with the payoff at 35-1 for a single number. The casino still has a 5.26% advantage.

Because the house has a built-in advantage, it wants the game to be played as honestly as possible. The roulette wheels, therefore, are built to be as friction-free as possible, so that there is no *bias* or deviation from a random situation prevailing. The wheels are inspected frequently and checked for any worn parts, such as pockets or dividers, since a worn part may create a bias.

Some players go from wheel to wheel, clocking them and checking out the pattern of numbers that come up, hoping for a bias. They rarely find one. If numbers seem to come up in any sequence out of the ordinary, it's probably coincidence. Even when there's a random sampling, numbers can repeat and appear to be in a strange sequence. Believe that the spins are still the result of chance.

The Roulette Layout

Now we come to the partner of the wheel at the roulette table: the layout. The layout contains all the possible betting situations that a player can use in roulette. The following is a typical roulette layout.

The layouts are usually green. The numbers from 1 through 36 are divided into three columns and are in numerical order. Each one is either red or black, corresponding to the colors on the wheel. 0 and 00 are at the head of the columns of numbers, and players may bet on them separately or together.

On the outside are the **even money bets**: 1-18, even, red, black, odd, and 19-36. Between them and the columns are the **dozens bets**: 1-12, 13-24, and 25-36, placed so that they correspond with the numbers in the columns. On the layout these dozens bets are marked, "1st 12," "2nd 12," and "3rd 12."

Finally we have the **columns bets**, which are at the far end of the columns, opposite the 0 and 00 areas. They each show 2-1, the price at which they are paid off. Each of these column areas covers all the numbers running down that column.

This layout is standard in American casinos. As we have said, it will accommodate all the possible bets that can be made at the roulette table.

		0		00
		1	2	3
1 to 18	1st 12	4	5	6
		7	8	9
EVEN		10	11	12
		13	14	15
◇	2nd 12	16	17	18
		19	20	21
◆		22	23	24
		25	26	27
ODD	3rd 12	28	29	30
		31	32	33
19 to 36		34	35	36
		2-1	2-1	2-1

III. Inside Bets

Because they take place within the thirty-six numbers, 0 and 00, the bets we'll be discussing in this section are called **inside** bets. With the exception of one bet, the Five-Number bet, which gives the house a 7.89% advantage, all the following wagers in American roulette give the house an edge of 5.26%.

3	6	9	12	15	18	21	24	27	30	33	36
2	5	8	11	14	17	20	23	26	29	32	35
1	4	7	10	13	16	19	22	25	28	31	34

Inside Bets

Let's begin with a favorite of roulette players the world over.

Straight-Up Bets
Single number bet; pays 35-1.

When a chip is placed on a single number, as shown on the layout below, this wager is called a **straight-up bet**. If the number comes up, the payoff is 35-1. If any other number comes up, including 0 or 00, the bet is lost.

A single number bet can be made on any number on the layout, including all numbers 1-36, as well as 0 and 00. No matter which number the player selects, the payoff will always be 35-1.

A player is not limited to one straight-up bet. He may make as many as he desires, and place as many chips on a single number (up to the house limit) as he wishes. For example, a player can put five chips on number 0, two on number 4, and one each on numbers 12, 15, 23, and 34.

No one will object, and since your chips will be a distinct color, they won't be confused with anyone else's.

To bet correctly, place your chip in the center of the numbered box, making sure not to touch any of the surrounding lines. If you touch the lines, you might have another kind of bet.

If another bettor likes your number and has placed a chip in that box, his wager doesn't preclude your making the same one. Simply place your chip (or chips) on top of the other player's. This is a perfectly valid way to bet. The house edge on such a bet is 5.26%.

Split Bets
Two numbers bet; pays 17-1.

In order to make a **split bet**, you should place your chip or chips on the line between two contiguous or adjacent numbers. On the layout, we see the chip placed between numbers 6 and 9 as a split bet, covering both numbers. The chip between 5 and 6 is also a split bet.

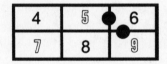

If either number comes up on a split bet, the player wins at 17-1. Split bets give the player double the chance to win, at just under half the payoff. Any two numbers may be split, as long as there is a line separating them. 0 and 00 may also be bet as a split number, either by putting a chip between these numbers, or, if you can't reach the 0 and 00 box, by putting one on the line between the second and third dozens.

Trio Bets
Three numbers bet; pays 11-1.

A **trio bet** can be made by placing a chip on the line separating the dozens betting area from the columns of numbers. The chip on the number 13 line in the layout below will cover the numbers 13, 14 and 15.

When a player makes a trio bet, he has covered three consecutive numbers. If any of those numbers comes up on the wheel, he receives a payoff of 11-1.

As you can see from the layout, the numbers that can be covered with a trio bet include 1, 2 and 3; 10, 11 and 12; 25, 26 and 27, and other similarly ordered groups.

The house advantage on this bet is still 5.26%

Corner Bets
Four numbers bet; pays 8-1.

A **corner bet** is made when a chip is placed at the point where four numbers converge, in exactly that corner. This type of bet is shown on the layout below, where the chip is placed between the numbers 23, 24, 26 and 27. If any of those numbers come up on the next spin of the wheel, the payoff will be 8-1. This wager is pretty versatile and can be used to cover various groups of four numbers, such as 2, 3, 5 and 6; 7, 8, 10 and 11; 22, 23, 25 and 26; and 32, 33, 35 and 36, among others.

The corner bet gives the house its usual 5.26% advantage.

Five-Number Bet
Five numbers bet; pays 6-1.

A **five-number bet** can be made only one way, and it covers the numbers 0, 00, 1, 2 and 3. A player makes such a bet by placing his chip at the convergence of the line separating the 0 and 00 and the line separating these numbers from the 1, 2 and 3. After noting where the chip goes, forget about this bet. It gives the house an advantage of 7.89%, and is therefore the *worst bet* on the entire roulette layout.

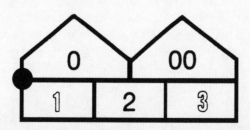

Since the French wheel contains only 0, not 00, this bet can't be made on that wheel. Take my advice—never make this bet at all.

Six-Number Bet

Six numbers bet; pays 5-1.

For a **six-number bet**, place the chip on the outside line separating the dozens bets from the inside numbers, at a point where this line crosses a line perpendicular to it that separates the six numbers we want to bet on. You can see an example of this bet in the layout diagrammed below.

In the diagram, this chip is placed so that the numbers 28, 29, 30, 31, 32 and 33 are covered. Thus one chip covers all six numbers. If any of those numbers hit, the bet will be paid off at 5-1.

There are eleven possible ways to make this six-number bet running up and down the side of the layout. Since a six-number bet covers so many numbers at once and yields a good 5-1 payoff, it's very popular among players.

The house edge on this wager is 5.26%.

A final note on these wagers: no matter how you make them and how many chips you risk, as long as you avoid the five-number bet, the house edge will never be anything other than 5.26%.

With all of these wagers, the player may make several bets of the same kind, covering several numbers. He may also make combinations of bets that cover as many numbers as he wishes, using as many chips as he cares to risk, provided that the total amount he bets is within the house limit on wagers.

IV. Outside Bets

The bets we'll now cover are made outside the 1-36, 0 and 00 numbered area. They are therefore considered **outside bets**.

There are three types of bets here. First, there are the even money wagers, then the dozens bets, and finally the column bets. We'll discuss each in turn.

1st 12		2nd 12		3rd 12	
1to18	EVEN	◇	◆	ODD	19to36

The Even Money Bets

There are three possible types of bets that one can make for even money: high-low, odd-even, or red-black. Of course, a player can make wagers on each of these choices, betting, for example, odd, red and high.

When a player bets on even money choices, the house wins automatically if the ball lands in the 0 or 00. There's one exception to this rule, and it takes place in Atlantic City or anywhere else where there's a **surrender rule**.

Let's discuss this rule now. If the number coming up is 0 or 00 in a place where surrender is allowed, the casino will allow you to remove *one-half of your bet*. In other words, you're surrendering just half your bet.

The European casinos go one step further. In those casinos, the rule in effect is called the **en prison rule**. You can either surrender half your bet, or you can allow your bet to be "imprisoned" for one more spin. If your choice then comes up, your bet stays intact. However, you don't win; you just get your bet back. In Atlantic City you can only surrender.

In the Nevada casinos, neither rule is in effect. There, if you bet on any even money choice and the 0 or 00 comes up, you're out of luck. You lose your bet outright.

High-Low Bets

The first of the even money bets we'll discuss is the **high-low bet**. You can bet high (19-36) or low (1-18). If you bet high and any number from 19 to 36 comes up, you win your bet at even money, or 1-1. If you bet low and any number from 1-18 comes up, again, you win even money.

Odd-Even

If you bet odd, then if any odd number comes up on the next spin of the wheel, you win your wager at even money, or 1-1. If you bet even, then similarly, if any even number comes up, your bet is paid off at even money. Remember, however, that the numbers 0 and 00 are losers for this kind of bet, just as they are for all bets which payoff at even money.

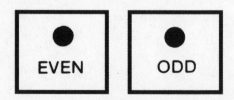

Red-Black

There are eighteen red numbers and eighteen black numbers, so the chances of a red or black number coming up on the next spin of the wheel are equal. If you bet on red, you will be paid off at even money, or 1-1, if a red number comes up. If you bet black, you win even money if a black number comes up.

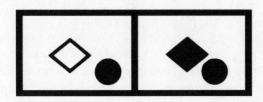

The layout diagrams show where you make your wagers for these even money choices. You can bet any amount up to the house limit, which is usually higher for even money choices than for the inside numbers, because the payoff is only at even money.

These even money choices are the heart of many roulette systems, and we'll cover a few in the later sections of this book. We'll show how they work, and we'll also explain their pitfalls.

Dozens Bets

These bets are paid off at 2-1, and there are three ways to bet them. You can bet on the first dozen, the second dozen or the third dozen. The first dozen covers numbers 1-12. On the layouts, it's often called the 1st 12. The numbers from 13-24 comprise the second dozen, which is known as the 2nd 12. Finally, there's the third dozen, from 25-36, which is known as the 3rd 12.

With each of those bets, a player is covering twelve numbers. Some players bet on two dozens at once, giving themselves twenty-four numbers. On these bets, as on the even-number wagers and the columns wagers, the house edge is always 5.26%.

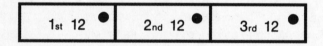

When a 0 or 00 comes up, you have an automatic loser. These numbers aren't included in the dozens bets, and there is no surrender or *en prison* rule covering them in any casino.

The layout diagram above shows how to make these wagers, and where to place the chip or chips you bet. The house limit on these bets is higher than those on the inside numbers.

Columns Bet

These bets are made at the head of each column directly opposite 0 and 00 on the layout. A bet on a particular column covers twelve numbers, some red and some black.

The payoff is at 2-1 for each column bet, but the 0 and 00 aren't included in any column. If they come up, your column bet is lost. There is no surrender or *en prison* rule on column wagers.

The house edge is 5.26% on all column bets.

We have discussed the *en prison* and surrender rules on even money wagers. The house edge without these rules is 5.26% on all even money wagers, as well as on the dozens and columns bets.

With the *en prison* and surrender rules, the house advantage drops to 2.70% *on only the even money wagers*.

Chart 1
Recapitulation of Bets and Payoffs

Single Number	35-1
Two Numbers	17-1
Three Numbers	11-1
Four Numbers	8-1
Five Numbers	6-1
Six Numbers	5-1
Column	2-1
Dozen	2-1
Odd-Even*	1-1
Red-Black*	1-1
High-Low*	1-1

All of the above bets give the house an advantage of 5.26%, except for the five-numbers bet, which gives the casino an advantage of 7.89%.
* When the surrender feature is allowed, the house advantage on these bets drops to 2.70%.

V. European Roulette

The European game and the American game are nearly the same. Besides the use of French terms, there are just two main differences. First, the European game uses only a single zero, in contrast to the zero and double zero played in America. Second, the European game incorporates the *en prison* rule.

Both the single zero and the *en prison* rule are beneficial to the players; they bring the casino advantage down to 1.35%.

The French wheel has spaces for thirty-seven numbers: the numerals 1-36, and the single 0. Red and black numbers alternate, but the placement of numbers is different than on the American wheel.

Like the American wheel, the French wheel contains a groove near its rim, where the *croupier* (dealer) places the ball, spinning it counter to the motion of the wheel. The ball hits metal buffers as it loses speed, and finally it falls into one of the pockets. Again, the pockets are separated from each other by metal sides.

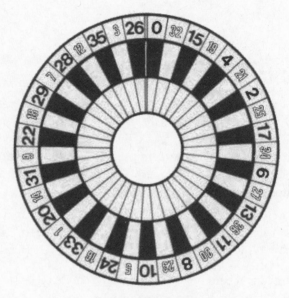

The French Wheel

The Layout

The European layout also differs from the American layout in two ways. The even money choices here are on opposite sides, rather than adjacent to each other. Also, the dozens bets can be made on two different sides of the layout. The wheel is above the box showing the 0.

Let's compare the European and the American bets, showing the different nomenclature.

Chart 2
European and American Nomenclature

American Bet	French Term	Odds
Straight-Up (One Number)	En plein	35-1
Split (Two Numbers)	A cheval	17-1
Trio (Three Numbers)	Transversale	11-1
Corner (Four Numbers)	Carre	8-1
Six Numbers	Sixain	5-1
* Red-Black	Rouge-Noir	1-1
* High-Low	Passe-Manque	1-1
*Odd-Even	Impair-Pair	1-1
Column	Colonne	2-1
Dozen	Douzaine	2-1

*The *en prison* rule is in effect for these bets only.

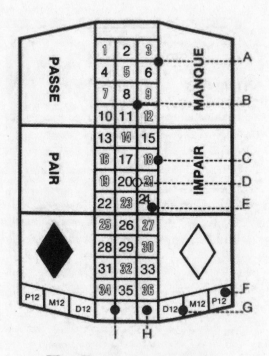

The European Layout

A. Transversale	6	numbers.
B. Carre	4	numbers.
C. Transversale	3	numbers.
D. Cheval	2	numbers.
E. Number, *en plein*	1	number.
F. Dozen	12	numbers.
G. Two dozens	24	numbers.
H. Column	12	numbers.
I. Two columns	24	numbers.

34

When you make dozens bets, you should realize that the first dozen (1-12) is marked as **P12** on the layout. The "P" stands for **Première**, a French word meaning "first." The second dozen (13-24) is called **M12**, for **Moyenne**, which means "middle." The third dozen is called **D12**, for **Derniére**, or "last."

To review, the *en prison* rule can be summarized as follows: when a 0 comes up on the wheel, the player's bet isn't lost. He now must make a choice: either he can surrender half his wager and keep the other half (a move known as **partage**), or his bet can be imprisoned for another spin, and, if it wins, he then loses nothing and gains nothing for that spin. To differentiate this second option from an ordinary wager, the player's chip or chips are placed on the line that borders the betting area.

Since the house advantage with the *en prison* rule is 1.35%, the most advantageous bets for players at a European casino would be on the even money choices.

There are many special bets also available at European casinos. Most of them involve what the French call **voisins**, or neighbors. A player can make a *voisins* bet on any number on the wheel, meaning that he would have bet on that number and on the two numbers on either side of it. Such a bet would be a five-chip bet. A **voisins du zero** bet involves a nine-chip bet, with eight chips bet on splits and one chip on the trio 0-2-3.

There are a handful of other wagers that are special to the European wheel, and you'll hear these referred to by names like *finals*, *les tiers*, and *les orphelins*.

These bets are rather complicated and tend to confuse beginning (and even some advanced) roulette players. We advise the player to concentrate instead on the even money choices and the simpler bets, such as corner bets or splits.

VI. Strategies & Systems at Roulette

Because of the high house edge at the American wheel without the surrender rule (an edge of 5.26% minimum on all bets), roulette at such casinos is not a game that you'll want to play for very serious money. The strong house advantage is quite difficult to overcome in the long run.

If you do play roulette, try to limit your losses. When you find yourself winning, try to make a good score and then quit while you're ahead. That's a philosophy that can't be beaten when gambling.

Getting Your Roulette Chips

When you first come to a table, you should ask the dealer what the minimum bets are at that particular table. If they're too high for your pocketbook, then don't play there.

Don't ever gamble with money you can't afford to lose, either financially or emotionally.

Different casinos have different minimum bet limits. They also have different standard valuations for their chips. When chips are valued at $1, a stack of twenty chips will cost you $20. Some casinos will value their chips at 50¢, in which case you pay just $10 for the same stack of twenty. Some casinos will even value their chips at a 25¢ standard, which means that a stack of twenty chips would cost you $5. You can figure out the standard valuation by finding out what a stack of chips will cost you.

If you feel comfortable with the amount of money you're going to risk, you should now ask the dealer about minimum bets. Find out the minimum bet allowed for the inside as well as the outside numbers. Remember, the inside numbers are all the numbers (from 1-36 plus the 0 and 00) that can be bet as one, two, three, four or six number bets. The outside bets are those that pay off at even money, plus the dozens and the columns wagers.

Even when the chips cost 25¢ each, the casino might require a minimum outside bet of $1, and a minimum inside bet of 25¢ on any choice but only with at least four chips in play at the same time. In other words, you won't necessarily be allowed to place just one chip on one inside betting proposition. You might have to put down at least four on one or several betting choices, which would mean that you'd be risking a dollar each spin after all.

These practices are fairly standard in casinos, so be sure that your bankroll can handle them. If you're at a table with a $1 valuation for the chips, and you must bet four (sometimes it's even five) chips at once on the inside propositions, then you may be out of your original stake after just a few losses.

What Bets to Make

If you're playing at a standard American table, with the 0 and 00 and no surrender rule, then all your bets will give the house the same advantage of 5.26% (except for the five-number wager—0, 00, 1, 2 and 3— where the house advantage is even higher). The higher the odds, the less likely you'll win. The lower the odds, the more often you'll win. Thus if you bet only on single numbers as straight-up bets, you'll get 35-1 for a win, but the odds are 37-1 against your winning.

On the other hand, if you bet on the even money choices, the odds against winning are only 20-18. You have 18 numbers working for you and 20 working against you, including the 0 and 00. Obviously you will theoretically win 18 out of 38 times, or much more often than 1 out of 37 times, as when betting a straight-up number.

The payoff is much less, of course: only even money. You must therefore use your discretion when making bets. Are you the type who wants to take a shot at a big payoff, or do you want to conserve your betting capital and hope to get a little bit ahead? It's your choice; the odds are the same where house percentage is concerned.

There are ways to compromise. You can make six-number bets and cover a large variety of numbers while still getting a good payoff. You can bet a key number straight-up, and then surround it with corner and trio bets. Many possibilities are available at the roulette table, and the choices are yours.

When you're playing at a table that allows surrender, you should by all means concentrate on the even money betting propositions. They cut the house edge in half, so why not take advantage? The same holds true when betting in a European game, since they incorporate the *en prison* rule. Bet on the even money choices. You get a second chance at winning back your bet when a 0 shows, and the house edge on this bet is down to 1.35%.

Betting Systems

The most well known, but also the most treacherous, systems to play are the Martingale and the Grand Martingale. The Martingale is often played by novices who feel that sooner or later their choice is going to come up, and to rationalize their bets, they call upon the *law of averages*.

Here's how the Martingale system works. It's really nothing more than a doubling up system. After a loss, you double your bet till you win.

For example, let's suppose you bet $1. You lose. Then you bet $2. You lose. You bet $4. You lose. You bet $8. You win.

Having won, you start all over again with a $1 wager. How much can you win with this system? Well, when you finish a sequence of doubling up with a win, you are ahead only $1.

Here's why:

Bet	Loss
$1	$1
$2	$3
$4	$7

At this point, you're behind $7. Then when you bet $8 and win, you win $8. Now you're ahead $1. Even if the bets escalate to $16, $32, $64, $128 and $256, when you finally win, you win $1. Imagine betting $256 to win $1! That's what this system is all about.

The Grand Martingale is even tougher. After each loss you add a unit to the bet, so that you win more than $1 when you finally win. The loss sequence, though, is $1, $3, $7, $15, and so forth, which can lead to astronomical losses in a very short time. If you're going to play these systems, you'd better have an awfully large bankroll to finance all your potential losses. It's better to avoid them.

The systems players who are die-hards think that the doubling up method will win because of the law of averages. After they've lost five bets on red, they feel that red is overdue because of the *law of averages*.

What they don't know is that there is no law of averages. There is only the law of large numbers, which roughly states that the more events played, the closer to the theoretical norm the result will be.

At the time the systems player is hoping for red to come up, he doesn't know that after a million spins of the wheel (even excluding the 0 and 00), red could have come up 521,202 times and black could have come up 478,798 times. Black still has a long way to go to catch up. In fact, it may never catch up, though it will come closer to the 50% norm as time goes by and there are several million more spins of the wheel.

If you want to play a betting system, play a very conservative one. For example, you might bet $1, and if it loses, bet $2. If that loses, you just want to break even, so you bet $3. If that loses, you've lost $6. You stop and restart with a $1 bet, hoping to win during the first two spins enough times to make up for the loss. Of course, you're not going to get rich that way, but you won't be losing your bankroll with one run of bad luck.

Since roulette is a leisurely game where you can sit down comfortably and make bets between spins of the wheel without much pressure, we suggest that you buy two stacks of chips and have fun playing. Hope to make some money through luck.

My best advice is to play some of your favorite numbers, make a few corner bets, and maybe some even number wagers. Enjoy yourself. If you have some luck, you can win big.

VII. More Winning Approaches

Bias of Wheels

Although, as we have shown, the game is one of pure chance governed by the law of averages, it is possible that some wheels may have a bias. By bias, we mean that there is something wrong with the wheel itself or with the mechanism of the wheel.

For example, the wheel may not be perfectly placed on a table, so that it tilts to one side ever so slightly, so slightly that the human eye can't detect this. But what happens is that the ball finds its way disproportionately into certain numbers more frequently. This can happen, especially in casinos where sloppy procedures in placing the wheel have been used.

Another bias may be found in the metal buffers which might get worn and will slow the ball down in other ways that pure chance. Or certain pockets might be worn and thus receptive to the ball.

After all, this is a device that is manufactured to certain exacting standards, but those standards may not hold up to the damage that repeated use of the wheel might inflict. Personnel in casinos can get sloppy, and not continually test the machine. Instead, the bias will continue.

If you are playing roulette at one of these machines, and you detect any such bias, then by all means take advantage of it.

A Bias Story

A habitué of the game told me that he was playing in a small casino in France and noticed that, under the glare of the chandelier, a few of the metal pockets gleamed unnaturally. They seemed to be more worn than others, and he clocked the wheel for an hour while making inconsequential wagers on the even-money choices.

Those worn pockets were attracting the ball more often than the other numbers, and he gradually started to make big bets on the four numbers that he had detected in this manner. He was rewarded with a huge profit for the evening.

He returned the next evening with the same good results. He made money for five straight nights, very serious money, and was dismayed to find that on the sixth night, the wheel had been replaced with a new one. Some executive of the casino had noticed something and replaced it.

My friend took the next plane back to London.

Winning Streaks

Although roulette is theoretically a game of pure chance, in which skill plays no part, there are times when everything seems to go the gambler's way. When this happens, it is wise to take advantage of this rush and increase your wagers.

Although most of the time you have to guess which numbers to play, or you simply play favorite numbers, there are other times when you can visualize what is going to happen. Whether it's ESP or some other kind of psychic intuition, the point is, it rarely happens, but it does happen. I can recall such a situation.

A Roulette Bonanza

I had arrived in London a few days earlier, and as a newcomer, you cannot simply go into a casino and gamble. The British authorities, in their purported wisdom, have a tight rule. You must show your passport to gain admittance, and must wait for 48 hours to play.

The rule is supposedly there to prevent a visitor to their fair country from impulsively gambling the moment he hits a casino. It seems to be a strange rule, for the same person impulsively gambles 48 hours later. But that's another story altogether.

I waited for 48 hours, which amounted really to two days and then went to this casino near Soho in the West End of London. It was a crowded smoky place, filled for the most part with foreigners, most of them Oriental or Asian. There were roulette wheels and blackjack tables.

I liked the European game of roulette with its en prison rule and single zero, and had done well in the past, so I decided to try my luck. I played for a few hours and won a little bit of money, about 50 pounds, then returned to my hotel at Knightsbridge, near Harrod's. The next day, I started talking to a lovely nurse who was from New Zealand, and who, like me, had just arrived a few days before in London. We made a date for dinner that evening and, after a sumptuous Chinese meal, I invited her to the gambling club for a bit of roulette.

At the club, she could enter without the 48 hour restriction as my guest, since I was now a bona fide member of the gambling establishment. We went to a roulette table after exchanging some pounds for chips.

I started with fifty pounds, my win the other night. I bet on some even-money choices and the table was choppy. I would win, lose, win and then lose, and in all I was down about five pounds when Alice, who now knew the game from my explanations and her observations, told me to make a bet on 29.

"Why?" I asked.

"I just have a feeling."

I bet three pounds on the number and was rewarded as the croupier called *vingt et neuf, noir, impair*, that is, 29, black and odd. I had won 105 pounds on the bet, and now hesitated. I took off the three pound bet and waited as the wheel spun around and the dealer placed the ball on the wheel.

"33," Alice cried.

I bet five pounds on 33. 12 won.

"Bet 33 again," she said, "I just have this feeling." So I bet another five pounds on 33, and it came up. 175 pounds was the payoff. I had now a net profit of 275 pounds from her numbers.

I didn't make a bet for the next three spins, then Alice told me to bet 14. I bet it and lost 10 pounds, bet again and lost another 10 pounds, and again lost 10 pounds.

However, on the fourth try, I was rewarded with a win. 14 had come up. 350 pounds was the win.

"How do you know what numbers to bet?" I asked her, as I stacked the chips in front of me.

"I just have this feeling."

"And you've never played roulette before?"

"Never, but sometimes I just feel things."

"Like what?" I asked.

"Play 9," she suddenly said. It came up five rolls later. And then I won again on 10, which she predicted.

Then the next number, 36, didn't come up, and after six futile bets, she suddenly said, "Let's get out of here. I can't stand to be in here anymore."

I cashed in and found that I had won 1,400 pounds. An amazing win in just over an hour's play, in which I hadn't even picked a number on my own.

"I could feel it leaving. It won't come back there anymore."

"What do you mean? You won't go back to the casino with me?"

"No, not me. It won't come back."

"What is it?" I asked.

"It's hard to explain. It's just something …." Her voice trailed off. "It was there and now it's gone. I can't really explain."

I'll always remember the "Kiwi" with the magical powers who made all that money for me in that London casino.

VIII. Clocking the Numbers

Using Pen and Pad

When playing roulette, it's a good idea to go to the table with a pen and pad, and keep track of the numbers as they come up on the wheel. In most casinos, that's the only way you can know which numbers have hit previously.

In many of the roulette games played nowadays, there's an automatic screen which lists the previous sixteen numbers. You may find this screen in other casinos, and the numbers shown are a big help to the player.

A Roulette Story

I recently clocked the numbers there and was not so surprised to find that three numbers had repeated in the last thirty-six number cycle. This may have been due to pure chance, or possibly a bias in the wheel, which is a real long shot.

Or it may have come from the habits of the croupier himself, who spun the ball at a certain speed and began his spin in various places, favoring some over others. Or the metal separators may have gotten worn from use, trapping the ball.

There was no instant way to find out, but I started on the numbers that had come up more than once. There were three of these numbers: 11, 24 and 31.

Clocking a 36-Game Cycle

Here's what I found: In the next 36-game cycle, the 11 came up three more times, and the 24 twice again, and the 27 just once.

By betting a dollar on these three numbers, I grossed $210. My losses were $102, giving me a net of $108. Not back at all. Now, I noticed that 28 had also come up twice, as did 6. So I changed my pattern of betting to now bet 6, 11, 24 and 28, saying adieu to the 27.

The 11 came up one more time, the 28 once more, and both the 6 and 24 missed altogether. The 27 came up once again, but I didn't have it. So, for the next 36 spins of the wheel, my gross win was $70, while I lost $142, for a net loss of $72.

I now studied the screen, which was, in reality, two separate columns of numbers placed above the table. The 11 and 28 had hit, as had the 27, which I lost faith in, and the 30 was now active, with two wins. So, for the next cycle, I bet a dollar on all these numbers. I was going with the flow.

I was rewarded. Good old 11 hit once, 27 hit twice more, 28 missed, but 30 was still hot, hitting twice in a row. Something was going on definitely with the 30. Now, at the end of that cycle of 36 spins, I had grossed $175, which dropping $139, for a net win of $36.

At that point, I called it a day, and added up my totals.

Gross wins: $455

Gross losses: $383

Net win: $72

Not bad for a wheel with two zeros. I now decided to look around for another wheel in another casino. I skipped the Strip hotels and found myself downtown, playing at a casino that shall remain nameless.

This one had no screen listing the previous wins of particular numbers, so I clocked them myself, betting a slight progression on red and black to pass the time and give myself something to root for.

Clocking a 40-Game Cycle

I clocked forty numbers and decided that would be my cycle. In the first forty number cycle, 10 hit three times, 17 twice and the rest were single wins, except for 00, which hit three times, rather spoiling my progression. So, I was ready.

I decided to bet $2 on each of these numbers, 00, 10 and 17. In the next forty roll cycle, the 00 stayed hot, hitting twice, and the 17 also hit twice, while the 10 hit once, but the 36, which I didn't have, hit four times.

So at the end of forty spins, I totaled up my wins

and losses. I had grossed $350 and lost $235, for a net win of $115.

I now studied the wheel closely while it was in spin. The room was rather dark, but I could see that certain metal pockets retained more of a shine than others, glinting a reflection off some distant light. Maybe they were more worn, who knows? I put my money where my instincts were.

I now bet $3 on 00, 10, 17 and added 36 to my little group. I was ready for another 40-spin cycle. For the first thirty rolls nothing happened.

I didn't hit once, and at $12 a pop, I was already down $360 for this wretched cycle. I decided, instead of quitting, to give it the ten more spins the cycle deserved. 00 came up, then 36, and right back to 00.

Then, after five misses, 00 hit again, as did 36 right afterwards. I was really onto something. At this point, I had grossed, during this cycle, the sum of $525. My losses were $465, for a win of $60.

So far, so good. I looked over my notepad. 18 had hit twice as had 19 and 25.

I decided to go all out for the next forty cycles of spins.

Taking a deep breath, I resolved to bet $5 per number. By this time a small crowd had gathered, for anytime a player hits numbers it looks exciting. I was betting pure numbers, not hedging the bets at all, and the payoffs looked good, with $25 chips being paid off.

My numbers were now 00, 36, and adding to these I put down 18, 19 and 25. At $5 a pop, I was betting

$25 each time the wheel spun around. At forty spins, that would be $1,000 down the drain if I didn't hit anything. Of course, each win was $175, and if I hit 6 times I'd be ahead.

We were off! The first six spins gave me nothing, then the good old 00 hit. And then, like clockwork, the 36 hit right afterwards. In the course of the forty spins, I hit four more times, twice with 18, once with 19 and once more with 36.

So I hit six times in the forty spins, giving me a gross win of $1,060. My losses were $970, for a net win of $80.

I was a bit washed up, but happy to be ahead for the session.

40-Game Cycle Win Analysis

Later, over coffee, I figured out what my chances were to win. In the simplest terms, if I played a forty number cycle, I was investing $1,000 by betting five numbers at $5 a shot.

I therefore had to win 5.714 times to break even, and since there was no such odd number of times to win at roulette, in reality, I needed six wins to come out ahead, which was what happened.

If I had bet four numbers, again at $5 a pop, it would cost me $800 for the full 40-spin cycle. With each win calculated at $175 ($35 x 5) I would have to win a theoretical 4.57 times to break even.

I calculated this down to a $1 bet. Still sticking with the 40 cycle spin, it comes out as follows:

Numbers Bet	Wins to Break Even
One	1.14
Two	2.28
Three	3.42
Four	4.57
Five	5.71
Six	6.85

In reality, each additional number bet has to win by a multiple of 1.14 in a forty-spin cycle to break even (actually, to be very slightly ahead).

Summary

I felt comfortable clocking the numbers and betting accordingly. I came out ahead in each session I played, and my luck has continued. I highly recommend this play rather than a random selection of numbers to bet.

It gives you a slight edge over other methods, especially if the croupier, wheel or something else is slightly out of whack, causing certain numbers to come up more frequently than others.

Roulette Tradition

Once you understand the game, and have the necessary funds, you can play the game anywhere it is legal to play. That is one of the beauties of roulette. It has attracted gamblers from the anonymous to the great. Winston Churchill loved to play roulette on the French Riviera and in Monte Carlo. When interviewed late in his great and illustrious life, he was asked if he had any regrets. His answer was succinct.

"Yes," the great leader replied, "I should have played red more often.

Thus, when you play roulette, you're following in the steps of many great personages who have been attracted and fascinated by this wonderful game.

IX. Money Management

Money management is always important in gambling. It means managing your gambling stake so that it not only can last a long time, but also will give you the chance of winning.

For purposes of playing roulette, I'd suggest getting two stacks of chips only if you can afford to take such a risk. Play with the standard valuations. Now you have forty chips to bet. To make them last, you might pick a few favorite numbers and cover them with corner or six-number bets, thus giving yourself a good chance of picking up a winning number.

At the same time, place a chip on two favorite numbers. If they hit, you're getting 35-1.

In the long run, try to double your original stake. If you can do that, you're doing well at roulette. You've made a nice win, and it's time to leave the table with your profits. If your luck turns the other way and you losechips back, then don't reach into your pocket for more cash.

Set your loss limits when you sit down at the table: two stacks and that's all you'll lose.

In this way, you'll have a shot at winning some money, some fun gambling, and not too much to lose.

Good luck!

X. Glossary

1st 12—The first twelve numbers on the layout, or 1-12. Known in French as **P12.**

2nd 12—The second twelve numbers on the layout, or 13-24. Known in French as **M12.**

3rd 12—The third twelve numbers on the layout, or 25-36. Known in French as **D12.**

American Wheel—The roulette wheel containing a 0 and 00.

Ball—The white, plastic object used in roulette, which is spun against the wheel's rotation to create a random spin.

Column Bet—A bet on one of the three columns on the roulette layout, each of which contains twelve numbers and is paid off at 2-1.

Combination Bet—A wager such as a corner bet, in which the bettor covers several inside numbers with just one chip or stack of chips.

Corner Bet—An inside bet in which the bettor uses one chip or stack of chips to cover four numbers at once. Also known as a **Four-Numbers Bet.**

Croupier—The French term for the employee who runs the roulette game.

D12—See **3rd 12**.

Derniére—The French word for "last."

Double Zero—See **Zero**.

Dozens Bet—A wager on either the first, second, or third dozen numbers on the layout.

En Prison Rule—A rule stating that when a 0 or 00 comes up, the player has the option of giving up half his bet or imprisoning the bet for one more spin. If the player's choice comes up on that next spin, nothing is won, but the bet is not lost. Also known as the **Surrender Rule**.

Even Money Bets—Bets paid off at even money, which include **High-Low**, **Odd-Even**, and **Red-Black**.

Five-Number Bet—A wager covering the 0, 00, 1, 2 and 3 which pays off at 6-1 and gives the house an advantage of 7.89%.

French Wheel—The standard wheel used in Europe, containing a single zero.

High-Low Bet—An even money bet that the next spin will come up either high (19-36) or low (1-18), depending on whether the bettor has wagered on high or low.

Inside Bet—A wager on any of the numbers, or combinations of numbers, including 0 and 00.

Layout—The printed surface showing all the wagers that can be made in roulette, on which players place their bets.

M12—See **2nd 12**.

Martingale System—A doubling-up system after each loss.

Moyenne—The French word for "middle."

Odd-Even Bet—An even money wager that the next spin will come up the way the player bet it, either an odd or even number.

Outside Bet—A wager on either the dozens, columns or even money choices.

P12—See **1st 12**.

Partage—A French term referring to the surrender of a bet under the *en prison* rule.

Première—The French word for "first."

Rake—A tool in European roulette used to collect and pay off chips.

Red-Black Bet—A wager paid off at even money on either the red or black numbers.

Separators—The metal dividers separating different pockets on the roulette wheel.

Six-Number Bet—A bet covering six inside numbers with one chip or stack of chips, paid off at 5-1.

Split Bet—A bet covering two numbers with one chip or stack of chips, paid off at 17-1.

Straight-Up Bet—A wager on just one number on the layout, paid off at 35-1.

Surrender Rule—See **En Prison Rule**.

Trio Bet—An inside bet covering three numbers at one time with one chip or stack of chips, paid off at 11-1.

Voisons—The French term for neighbors, referring to neighboring numbers on the French wheel.

Voisons du Zero—A nine-chip bet involving splits and 0-2-3.

Zero, Double Zero—Numbers on the wheel in addition to the regular 1-36 numerals; these allow the casino to have an edge over the players. Also called **House Numbers**.

LOTTERY SUPER SYSTEM
LotterySuperSystem.com

WIN MONEY PLAYING THE LOTTERY—FINALLY!

Lottery Super System is jam packed with super-charged strategies specifically designed to beat the lotto and lottery. Based on Prof. Jones Gold and Platinum lotto and lottery systems, and now fully upgraded, expanded and modernized for today's games, Lottery Super System is the result of thirty years of intense scientific research and testing, and the result is the most powerful arsenal of winning programs ever developed.

FIVE POWER STRATEGIES ARE INCLUDED!

The heart of Lottery Super System engine is its five power strategies—a formidable 100 game regression analysis (plus models with even stronger engines), best number analysis, overdue analysis, cluster analysis, and lucky number analysis. Also included are full computer-generated wheeling systems to optimize all your bets into the specified number of lotto and lottery tickets you choose. We also include an instructional guide on how to use our wheeling systems to win millions and millions of dollars. Lottery Super System contains individual modules optimized for all 3 ball, 4 ball, 5 ball, and 6 ball lotto and lottery games from 6/49 to 6/54, multistate games such as Power Ball, and every major lottery and lotto game.

EXOTIC SYSTEMS & FREE BONUS E-REPORT!

Lottery Super System features all the bells, whistles and goodies you expect from a premier power program, *and* includes exotic wagering systems for bettors who don't follow the pack. You also get plus a free bonus e-report ($37.99 value), *The Secrets of Using Core Numbers to Wheel a Fortune*. With constant upgrades, you've always got the latest tools at your disposal

WIN $10,000,000 OR MORE PLAYING THE LOTTERY!!!

Imagine if you win $10,000,000! It could happen, and it could happen to you! Maybe you'll win less, maybe even more. But one thing we can promise you: Your chances of winning small jackpots and big million-dollar jackpots will immediately double, triple, and even increase tenfold! Sound too good to be true? Go to our website now to get all your questions answered and to see all the features of this winning program and how it can instantly increase your chances of winning results!

LotterySuperSystem.com
Go Online Now!

Baccarat Master Card Counter
NEW WINNING STRATEGY!

For the **first time**, Gambling Research Institute releases the **latest winning techniques** at baccarat. This **exciting** strategy, played by big money players in Monte Carlo and other exclusive locations, is based on principles that have made insiders and pros **hundreds of thousands of dollars** counting cards at blackjack - card counting!

NEW WINNING APPROACH

This brand **new** strategy now applies card counting to baccarat to give you a **new winning approach,** and is designed so that any player, with just a little effort, can successfully take on the casinos at their own game - and win!

SIMPLE TO USE, EASY TO MASTER

You learn how to count cards for baccarat without the mental effort needed for blackjack! No need to memorize numbers - keep the count on the scorepad. Easy-to-use, play the strategy while enjoying the game!

LEARN WHEN TO BET BANKER, WHEN TO BET PLAYER

No longer will you make bets on hunches and guesses - use the GRI Baccarat Master Card Counter to determine when to bet Player and when to bet Banker. You learn the basic counts (running and true), deck favorability, when to increase bets and much more in this **winning strategy**.

LEARN TO WIN IN JUST ONE SITTING

That's right! After **just one sitting** you'll be able to successfully learn this powerhouse strategy and use it to your advantage at the baccarat table. Be the best baccarat player at the table - the one playing the odds to **win**! Baccarat can be beaten. The Master Card Counter shows you how!

To order, send $50 by bank check or money order to:
Cardoza Publishing.P.O. Box 1500, Cooper Station, New York, NY 10276

WIN MONEY AT BACCARAT!

I want to learn the latest winning techniques at baccarat. Please rush me the **GRI Baccarat Master Card Counter** and **Free Bonus**. Enclosed is a check or money order for $50 (plus postage and handling) to:

Cardoza Publishing
P.O. Box 98115, Las Vegas, NV 89193
Call Toll-Free in U.S. & Canada, 1-800-577-WINS

Include $5.00 postage and handling for U.S. & Canada, other countries $10.00. Orders outside U.S., money order payable in U.S. dollars on U.S. bank only.

NAME _____

ADDRESS _____

CITY _____ STATE _____ ZIP _____

Order Now! - 30 Day Money Back Guarantee!   GRI RO 15